SCHOLASTIC

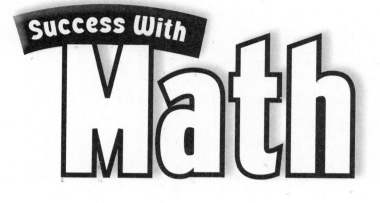

Success With Math

New York • Toronto • London • Auckland • Sydney
Mexico City • New Delhi • Hong Kong • Buenos Aires

Teaching *Resources*

State Standards Correlations

To find out how this book helps you meet your state's standards, log on to **www.scholastic.com/ssw**

Cover design by Ka-Yeon Kim-Li
Interior design by Ellen Matlach Hassell
for Boultinghouse & Boultinghouse, Inc.

ISBN 978-0-545-20069-1

Contents

"Nothing succeeds like success."
—Alexandre Dumas the Elder, 1854

And no other math resource helps kids succeed like *Scholastic Success With Math!* For classroom or at-home use, this exciting series for kids in grades 1 through 5 provides invaluable reinforcement and practice for math skills such as:

❑ number sense and concepts
❑ reasoning and logic
❑ basic operations and computations
❑ story problems and equations
❑ time, money, and measurement
❑ fractions, decimals, and percentages
❑ geometry and basic shapes
❑ graphs, charts, tables . . . and more!

This 64-page book contains loads of challenging puzzles, riddles, inviting games, and clever practice pages to keep kids delighted and excited as they strengthen their basic math skills.

What makes *Scholastic Success With Math* so solid?

Each practice page in the series reinforces a specific, age-appropriate skill as outlined in standardized tests. These skills help kids succeed in daily math work and on standardized achievement tests. And the handy Instant Skills Index at the back of the book helps you zero in on the skills your kids need most!

Cow Code

Name _____ Date _____

Riddle: Where do cows go for entertainment?

What to Do

Find the corresponding numerals below. Then use the Decoder to solve the riddle by filling in the spaces at the bottom of the page.

❶ nine _____

❷ twenty-two _____

❸ seventeen _____

❹ forty-five _____

❺ sixty-seven _____

❻ one hundred eight _____

❼ eighty-six _____

❽ one hundred fifty-three _____

❾ three hundred seventy _____

❿ five hundred thirty-four _____

Decoder

23 X
17 .... O
153 .... E
21 .... A
370 .... O
108 .... S
76 .... D
9 V
15 .... F
67 .... T
22 .... E
435 .... P
86 .... H
88 .... R
45 I
534 .... M
118 .... W
543 .... N
307 .... G

TO __ __ __ " __ __ __ __ __ __ __ "
   5 7 2   10 3 9   1 4 8 6

Space Chase Place Value

Use strategies to capture creepy space creatures while learning about place value.

You'll Need

For each pair:
◆ Space Chase Place Value (page 7)
◆ Paper clip
◆ Pencils

Directions

1. Review place value to the hundred thousands place. You will need this knowledge if you want to do well in the Space Chase game.

2. Partner up with a classmate, friend, or family member. To make your own spinner, spin a paper clip around a pencil placed at the spinner's center. Players should spin to see who goes first, with the higher spin going first. Players then take turns spinning.

3. On each turn, a player spins and lands on a number. The player then says which creepy space creature he or she will capture on that turn. Players write the number they landed on in the blank that corresponds with the place value of the space creature. (For example: In round 1, Player 1 spins a 5. She decides to capture a Kerpew on this turn. Kerpews represent the ten thousands place. So Player 1 writes a 5 in the ten thousands place of her Round 1 score blanks.) Players record their numbers in the score blanks of the round they are playing.

4. A particular space creature can be captured only once per round. The round ends when both players have captured all six space creatures. Play continues for three rounds. The winner of each round is the player who has written the greater 6-digit number.

Space Chase Place Value

Name _____ Date _____

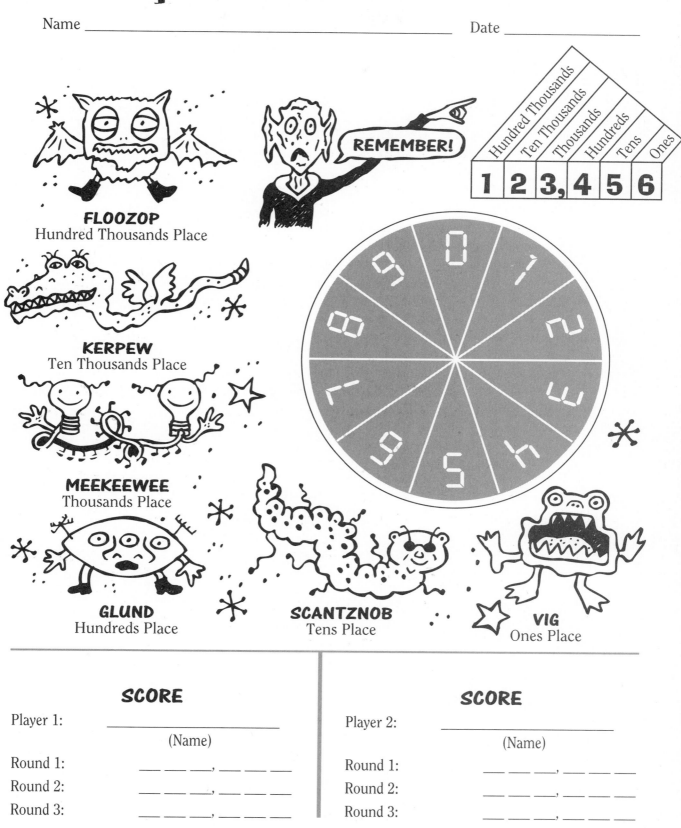

Hundred Thousands	Ten Thousands	Thousands	Hundreds	Tens	Ones
1	2	3,	4	5	6

REMEMBER!

FLOOZOP
Hundred Thousands Place

KERPEW
Ten Thousands Place

MEEKEEWEE
Thousands Place

GLUND
Hundreds Place

SCANTZNOB
Tens Place

VIG
Ones Place

SCORE

Player 1: _____
(Name)

Round 1: __ __ __ , __ __ __
Round 2: __ __ __ , __ __ __
Round 3: __ __ __ , __ __ __

SCORE

Player 2: _____
(Name)

Round 1: __ __ __ , __ __ __
Round 2: __ __ __ , __ __ __
Round 3: __ __ __ , __ __ __

Newspaper Math

Name _____ Date _____

What to Do:

Use a newspaper to find the numbers listed below. Cut out your answers from the newspaper and tape them in the box with each question.

> **EXTRA! EXTRA!**
> **Read All About It!**

1. From the weather report, find the temperature in two cities.

2. Pick three items advertised for sale.

3. Find two different times that the same movie is playing.

4. From the TV listings, pick three programs that you would like to watch. Include the channels that those programs will be on.

5. Choose two numbers from an article of your choice.

Place-Value Puzzler

Name _____ Date _____

What is too much fun for one, enough for two, and means nothing to three?

Find the answer to this riddle by using place value! Take a look at each number below. One digit in each number is underlined. Circle the word in each line that tells the place value of the underlined number. Write the letters next to each correct answer in the blanks below. The first one is done for you.

A.	1<u>5</u>,209	**a** thousands	**i** hundreds
B.	4,7<u>2</u>9	**n** hundreds	**s** tens
C.	<u>4</u>25	**e** hundreds	**o** tens
D.	7,6<u>1</u>8	**c** tens	**g** ones
E.	1,<u>1</u>12	**p** thousands	**r** hundreds
F.	8,63<u>6</u>	**a** hundreds	**e** ones
G.	2<u>2</u>2	**t** tens	**m** ones

a
___   ___ ___ ___ ___ ___ ___
A   B   C   D   E   F   G

Bee Riddle

Name _____ Date _____

Riddle: What did the farmer get when he tried to reach the beehive?

Round each number. Then use the Decoder to solve the riddle by filling in the spaces at the bottom of the page.

Decoder

400	**A**
800	**W**
30	**O**
10	**Y**
25	**E**
500	**I**
210	**J**
20	**L**
40	**C**
700	**U**
90	**S**
100	**T**
600	**G**
95	**F**
50	**N**
550	**V**
300	**Z**
7	**H**
200	**Z**

❶ Round 7 to the nearest ten _____

❷ Round 23 to the nearest ten _____

❸ Round 46 to the nearest ten _____

❹ Round 92 to the nearest ten _____

❺ Round 203 to the nearest hundred _____

❻ Round 420 to the nearest hundred _____

❼ Round 588 to the nearest hundred _____

❽ Round 312 to the nearest hundred _____

❾ Round 549 to the nearest hundred _____

❿ Round 710 to the nearest hundred _____

A "B __ __ __ __ " __ __ __ __ __ __

   10   5   8   1   4   9   7   3   6   2

Discover Coordinates!

Name _____ Date _____

Follow the coordinates to the correct box, then draw in the underlined treasures on this treasure map.

C3 A <u>jeweled crown</u> sparkles.

B1 A <u>ruby necklace</u> can be found.

C5 A <u>golden cup</u> awaits you.

D4 An <u>X</u> marks the spot!

A4 A <u>wooden treasure chest</u> you'll find.

E1 A <u>silvery sword</u> lies here.

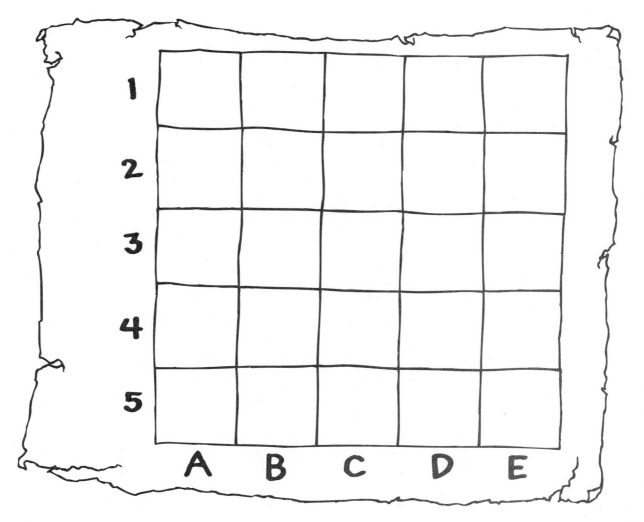

11

Tropical Tree

Name _____ Date _____

1. Solve the problems.

2. Find each number pair on the graph. Make a dot for each.

3. Connect the dots in the order that you make them.

4. What picture did you make?

_____

	Across	Up
1.	10 – 5 = _____	7 – 0 = _____
2.	19 – 12 = _____	9 – 4 = _____
3.	10 – 4 = _____	18 – 11 = _____
4.	20 – 12 = _____	8 – 2 = _____
5.	9 – 3 = _____	17 – 9 = _____
6.	18 – 10 = _____	15 – 8 = _____

	Across	Up
7.	17 – 11 = _____	19 – 10 = _____
8.	20 – 16 = _____	11 – 2 = _____
9.	19 – 18 = _____	13 – 5 = _____
10.	20 – 17 = _____	15 – 7 = _____
11.	20 – 19 = _____	14 – 8 = _____
12.	18 – 15 = _____	20 – 13 = _____
13.	13 – 12 = _____	16 – 11 = _____
14.	17 – 13 = _____	16 – 9 = _____

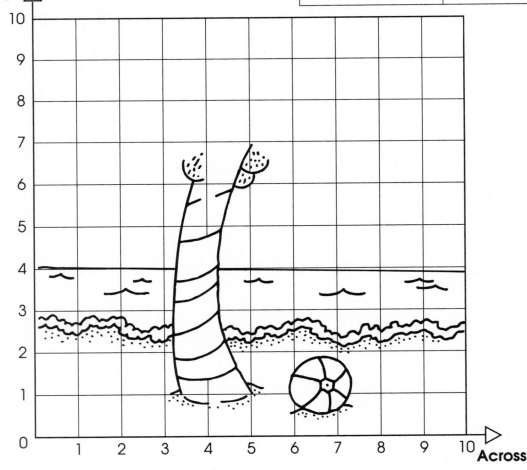

12

Animal Caller

Name _____ Date _____

A bar graph shows information. This bar graph shows the speeds of animals in miles per hour. Use the graph to answer the questions.

WHICH ANIMAL IS...

1. THE FASTEST?

_____

2. THE SLOWEST?

_____

3. GOING 40 mph?

_____

4. 20 mph FASTER THAN A CAT?

_____

5. HOW MANY 4-FOOTED ANIMALS ARE LISTED?

_____

DO THE BARS SHOW...

6. ANIMAL NAMES AND mph?

_____

7. SPEED OR WEIGHT?

_____

8. INFORMATION ABOUT TIGERS?

_____

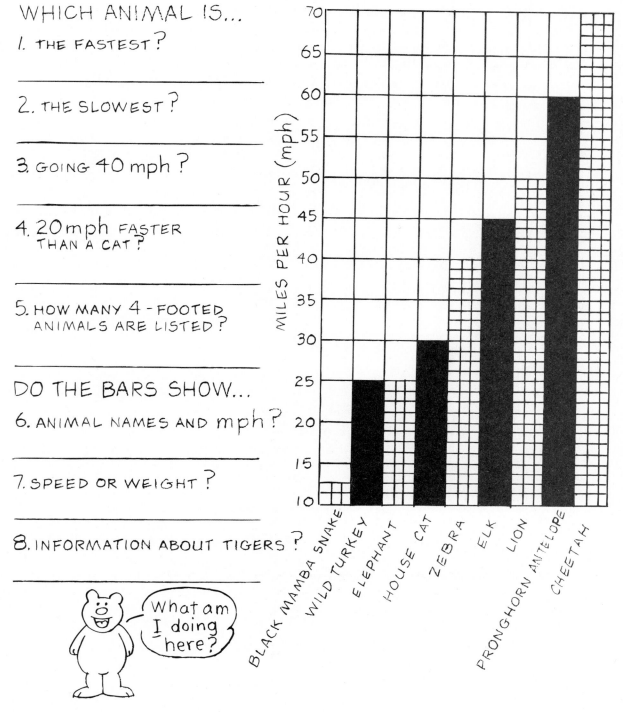

What am I doing here?

Great Graphing

Name _____ Date _____

How many pennies equal 5¢? How many nickels equal 5¢? Color in the boxes on the graph to show your answer.

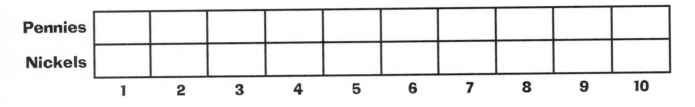

How many pennies equal 10¢? How many nickels equal 10¢? How many dimes equal 10¢? Color in the boxes on the graph to show your answer.

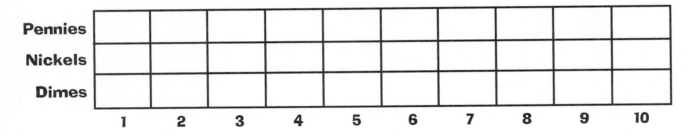

How many pennies equal 25¢? How many nickels equal 25¢? How many quarters equal 25¢? Color in the boxes on the graph to show your answer.

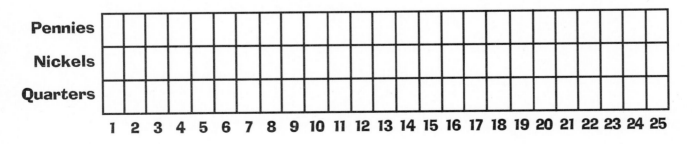

14

Graph Drafter

Name _____ Date _____

A line graph shows how something changes over time. This line graph shows temperature changes during a year in New York City. Use the graph to answer the questions below.

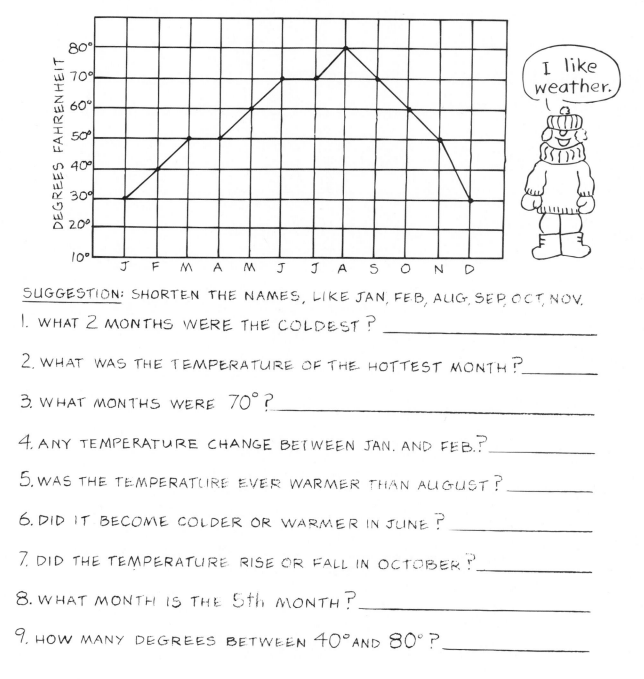

SUGGESTION: SHORTEN THE NAMES, LIKE JAN, FEB, AUG, SEP, OCT, NOV.

1. WHAT 2 MONTHS WERE THE COLDEST? _____

2. WHAT WAS THE TEMPERATURE OF THE HOTTEST MONTH? _____

3. WHAT MONTHS WERE 70°? _____

4. ANY TEMPERATURE CHANGE BETWEEN JAN. AND FEB.? _____

5. WAS THE TEMPERATURE EVER WARMER THAN AUGUST? _____

6. DID IT BECOME COLDER OR WARMER IN JUNE? _____

7. DID THE TEMPERATURE RISE OR FALL IN OCTOBER? _____

8. WHAT MONTH IS THE 5th MONTH? _____

9. HOW MANY DEGREES BETWEEN 40° AND 80°? _____

Menu Math

Name _____ Date _____

Good Morning!

Use the menu on the following page to answer the following questions.

1. Which hearty breakfast costs the most? _____
   Which one costs the least? _____

2. Mary orders French toast and juice.
   What does her meal cost? _____

3. Hiram orders Irish oatmeal, a bagel, and juice.
   What is the cost of his meal? _____

4. Jack orders tortillas and eggs and hot cocoa. Danielle orders
   Chinese breakfast rice, sausage, and milk.
   Who spends more? _____
   How much more? _____

5. Paco orders a hearty breakfast with home fries and juice. His meal
   costs $7.50. Which hearty breakfast does he order?

   _____

6. You have $8 to spend at the cafe! Order a hearty breakfast, a side
   dish, and a drink.
   What does your whole meal cost? _____
   What is your change? _____

Hearty Breakfasts

Irish Oatmeal $2.50

Swedish Pancakes $3.50

French Toast $3.50

Tortillas and Eggs $4.00

Chinese Breakfast Rice $2.00

Eggs Your Way $2.50

Tropical Fruit & Yogurt $3.00

Side Dishes

Bagel $1.50

Biscuits $1.00

English Muffin $1.00

Navajo Fry Bread $1.50

Home Fries $1.50

Grits $1.00

Bacon or Sausage $2.00

Drinks

Milk $1.50

Hot Cocoa $2.00

Juice $2.00

Tea $1.00

Plus & Minus Puzzle

Name _____ Date _____

☞ In this crossnumber puzzle, your mission is to answer these addition and subtraction problems. So you don't get boxed in, we did the first one for you!

$$\begin{array}{r} 243 \\ -\ 126 \\ \hline 117 \end{array}$$

ACROSS:

A. 243 – 126
C. 96 – 8
E. 105 – 38
F. 18 + 6
G. 65 – 36
H. 43 + 28
I. 234 + 323
K. 53 + 9
L. 84 – 16
N. 134 – 43
O. 80 – 46

DOWN:

A. 455 – 313
B. 41 + 34
C. 624 + 238
D. 5526 + 3264
H. 169 – 92
I. 39 + 17
J. 600 – 71
L. 41 + 22
M. 65 + 19

Using this grid, create your very own crossnumber puzzle. Make up your own addition and subtraction problems. Ask a classmate to complete your puzzle.

Stretching Taffy

Name _____ Date _____

Solve the problems. Then connect the dot below each problem on Line A to the dot beside its answer on Line C. The first line has been drawn for you. Connect the dot above each problem on Line B to the dot beside its answer on Line C. Some dots on Line C will not be used.

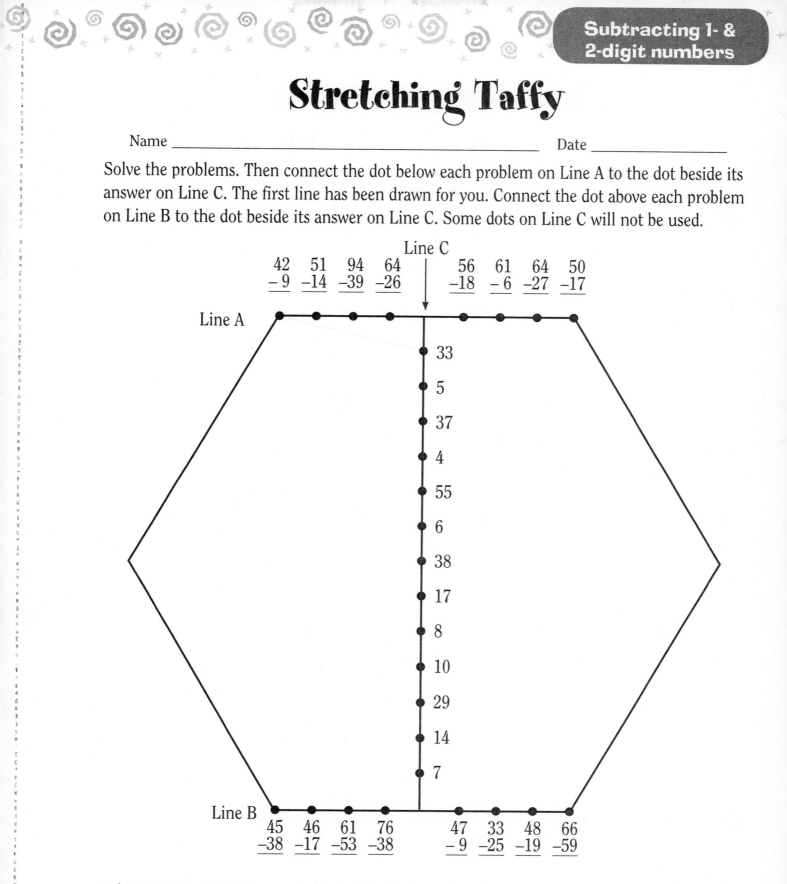

Line C

$$42 \atop -9 \qquad 51 \atop -14 \qquad 94 \atop -39 \qquad 64 \atop -26 \qquad 56 \atop -18 \qquad 61 \atop -6 \qquad 64 \atop -27 \qquad 50 \atop -17$$

Line A

33
5
37
4
55
6
38
17
8
10
29
14
7

Line B

$$45 \atop -38 \qquad 46 \atop -17 \qquad 61 \atop -53 \qquad 76 \atop -38 \qquad 47 \atop -9 \qquad 33 \atop -25 \qquad 48 \atop -19 \qquad 66 \atop -59$$

Taking It Further: Amanda picked 9 flowers from her garden and added them to some flowers in a vase. Now she has 16 flowers in all. How many flowers were in the vase to begin with? _____

19

Riddle Subtraction

Name _____ Date _____

To find the answers to the riddles, solve the math problems. Write one number on each blank. The first one has been done for you. Then write the letters under each line in the boxes above that have the same number. When you have filled in all of the boxes with the right letters, you'll find out the answers to the riddles.

What has hands, but no feet and runs all day?

| 1. | | 2. | 3. | 4. | 5. | 6. |

```
  60        52        64
 -34       -38       -29
 ____      ____      ____
  2  6      _  _      _  _
  C  K      A  O      L  C
```

Where can you find cards on a ship?

| 1. | 2. | | 3. | 4. | 5. | 6. |

```
  44        51        70
 -28       -26       -36
 ____      ____      ____
  _  _      _  _      _  _
  O  K      N  C      D  E
```

What bird can lift the most weight?

| 1. | | 2. | 3. | 4. | 5. | 6. |

```
  41        64        81
 -29       -28       -36
 ____      ____      ____
  _  _      _  _      _  _
  A  C      R  E      A  N
```

What breaks when you say its name?

| 1. | 2. | 3. | 4. | 5. | 6. | E |

```
  80        91        92
 -49       -49       -36
 ____      ____      ____
  _  _      _  _      _  _
  L  S      E  I      N  C
```

Morning Glory

Name _____ Date _____

Solve the problems. If the answer is between 0 and 250, color the shape yellow.

If the answer is between 251 and 500, color the shape purple.

If the answer is between 501 and 1,000, color the shape pink.

Finish the design by coloring the other shapes with the colors of your choice.

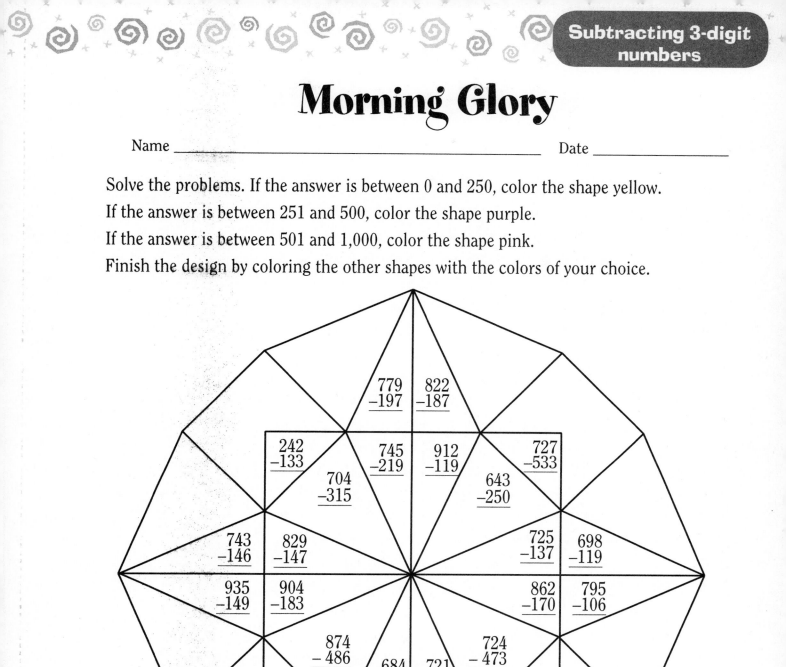

Taking It Further: Arrange the digits 7, 3, and 9 to make the largest number possible. Then rearrange them to make the smallest number possible. Subtract the smaller number from the larger number. Write your answer here: _____ .

21

Eager Achiever

Name _____ Date _____

Fill in the missing numbers.

```
  5 □ 9
-   □ 3 □
  3 0 4
```

```
  5 □ 5
- 4 6 8
  □ 0 □
```

```
  5 □ 3
- □ 4 □
  2 2 1
```

```
  9 □ □
- 8 4 1
  □ 4 3
```

```
  6 5 3
- □ 2 □
  1 □ 6
```

```
  3 3 □
- 2 □ 6
  □ 0 3
```

They won't let me subtract yet.

```
  □ 3 □
- 4 □ 7
  □ 1 8
```

```
  7 □ □
- 2 2 5
  □ 4 3
```

```
  □ 8 6
- 2 5 □
  2 □ 9
```

```
  8 5 0
- □ □ □
  5 2 6
```

Clowning Around

Name _____ Date _____

At Arnold's Circus, all of the clowns dress alike. But there are really only two clowns that are exactly the same. Can you find them? Check your answer by solving the subtraction problem under each clown. The identical clowns have the same answer.

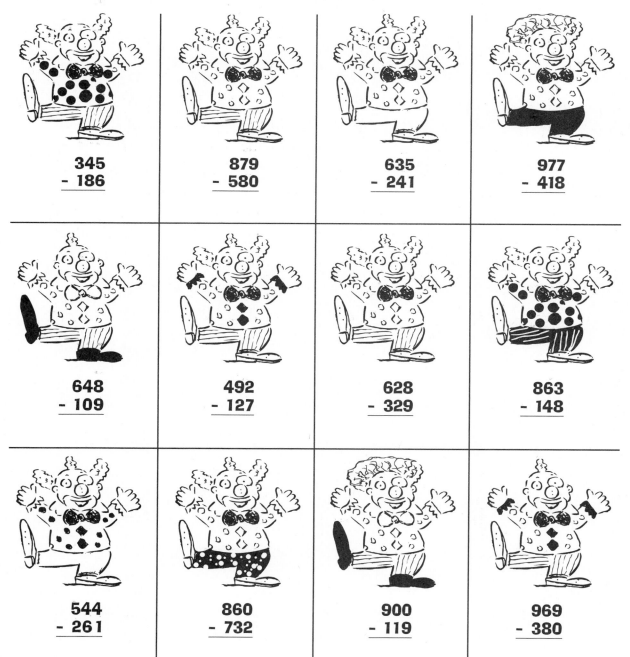

345 − 186	879 − 580	635 − 241	977 − 418
648 − 109	492 − 127	628 − 329	863 − 148
544 − 261	860 − 732	900 − 119	969 − 380

Freebie Fun

Name _____   Date _____

What does a basketball player
never have to pay for?

What to Do

To find the answer to the riddle,
solve the multiplication problems.
Then, match each product with a
letter in the Key below. Write the
correct letters on the blanks below.

1   **3 x 4** = _____   **6**   **10 x 4** = _____

2   **6 x 4** = _____   **7**   **8 x 4** = _____

3   **2 x 4** = _____   **8**   **13 x 4** = _____

4   **9 x 4** = _____   **9**   **1 x 4** = _____

5   **7 x 4** = _____   **10** **12 x 4** = _____

Key

11 I		48 .... R		23 .... G	
24 .... E		40 .... A		32 .... W	
36 .... H		52 .... F		4 .... E	
28 .... R		7 .... N		50 .... D	
12 .... T		8 .... O		22 C	

Riddle
Answer:

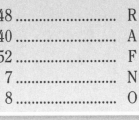

" _____ _____ _____ _____ _____ " _____ _____ _____ _____ _____
 6   **8 5 2 9**   **1 4 10 3 7**

Fall Is in the Air!

Name _____ Date _____

Crunch, crunch, crunch! Do the multiplication problems; then follow the path of leaves to the haystack. Move one leaf at a time in any direction except diagonally. You can only step on leaves that contain odd-numbered answers. Draw a line to show your path.

Friendship

Name _____ Date _____

You always have something to give a friend. What is it? _____

To find the answer, do the multiplication problems and then follow the directions below.

   Color the squares in row 1 that contain even answers.

   Color the squares in row 2 that contain odd-numbered answers.

   Color the squares in row 3 that contain answers greater than 30 and less than 40.

   Color the squares in row 4 that contain answers greater than 50 and less than 60.

   Color the squares in row 5 that contain odd-numbered answers.

The letters in the colored squares spell the answer.

$\begin{array}{r}6\\ \times 1\end{array}$	$\begin{array}{r}6\\ \times 4\end{array}$	$\begin{array}{r}7\\ \times 7\end{array}$	$\begin{array}{r}6\\ \times 2\end{array}$
Y	**O**	**T**	**U**
$\begin{array}{r}7\\ \times 9\end{array}$	$\begin{array}{r}6\\ \times 3\end{array}$	$\begin{array}{r}7\\ \times 3\end{array}$	$\begin{array}{r}7\\ \times 6\end{array}$
R	**W**	**S**	**O**
$\begin{array}{r}7\\ \times 4\end{array}$	$\begin{array}{r}6\\ \times 5\end{array}$	$\begin{array}{r}6\\ \times 6\end{array}$	$\begin{array}{r}6\\ \times 9\end{array}$
C	**E**	**M**	**L**
$\begin{array}{r}7\\ \times 8\end{array}$	$\begin{array}{r}7\\ \times 0\end{array}$	$\begin{array}{r}6\\ \times 7\end{array}$	$\begin{array}{r}6\\ \times 0\end{array}$
I	**F**	**R**	**B**
$\begin{array}{r}7\\ \times 5\end{array}$	$\begin{array}{r}6\\ \times 8\end{array}$	$\begin{array}{r}7\\ \times 2\end{array}$	$\begin{array}{r}7\\ \times 1\end{array}$
L	**J**	**S**	**E**

Rainy Day

Name _____ Date _____

Solve the problems. Then connect the dot beside each problem to the dot beside its answer on Line A. One line has been drawn for you. Some dots on Line A will not be used.

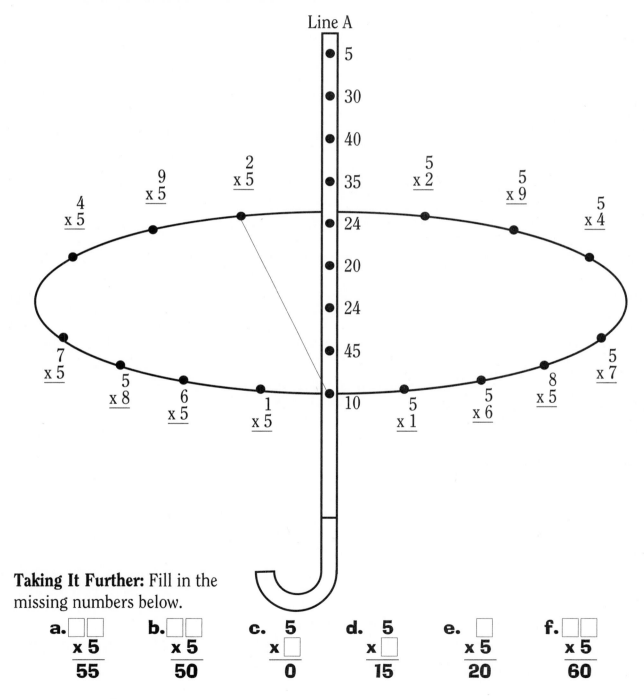

Taking It Further: Fill in the missing numbers below.

a. □□
    x 5
    ─────
    55

b. □□
    x 5
    ─────
    50

c. 5
    x □
    ─────
    0

d. 5
    x □
    ─────
    15

e. □
    x 5
    ─────
    20

f. □□
    x 5
    ─────
    60

Space Traveler

Name _____ Date _____

Solve the problems. If the answer is between 0 and 45, color the shape black.
If the answer is between 46 and 85, color the shape red.
Finish the design by coloring the other shapes with the colors of your choice.

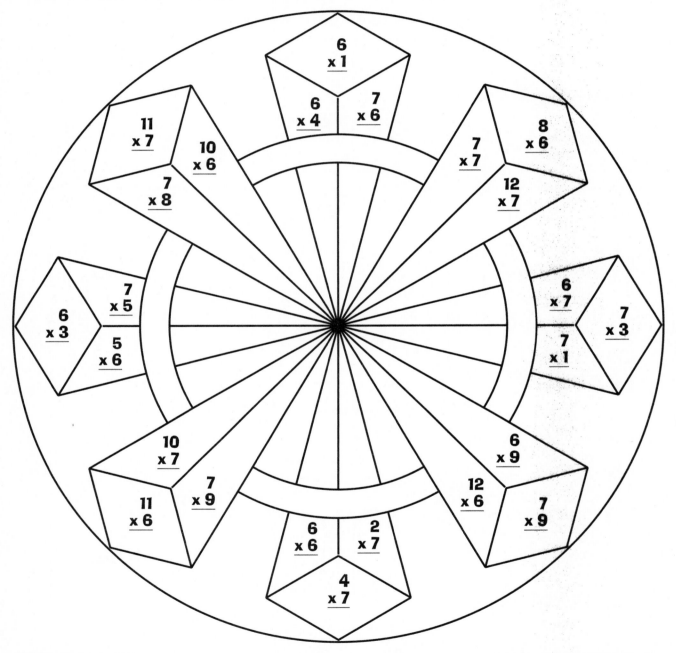

Taking It Further: Look at the four numbers below. Which two numbers, when multiplied together, are greater than 200 but less than 400? 4, 8, 23, 49 _____

Introducing division with remainders

Eager Seeker

Name _____ Date _____

Divide the objects and food equally among the groups of people shown below. How many will each person receive? How much will be left over?

ITEM	NUMBER OF PEOPLE	EACH	LEFT OVER
1. 28 MARBLES			
2. 15 STICKS OF BUBBLE GUM			
3. 8 ONE DOLLAR BILLS			
4. 15 SLICES OF PIZZA			
5. 4 BALLOONS			
6. 25 MARSHMALLOWS			
7. 6 TOY DINOSAURS			
8. 29 FRENCH FRIES			
9. 12 STRAWBERRIES			
10. 19 COOKIES			

29

Exploding Star

Name _____ Date _____

Solve the problems. If the answer is even, color the shape blue.
If the answer is odd, color the shape orange.

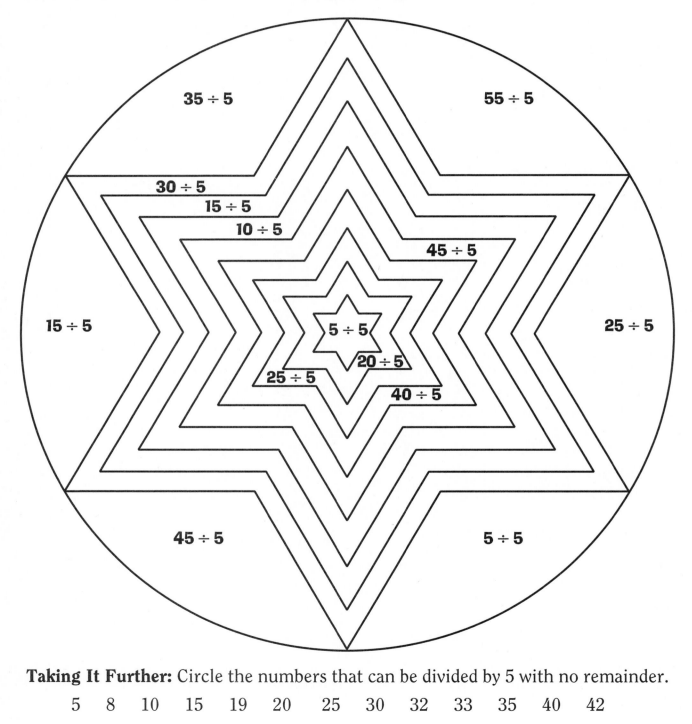

Taking It Further: Circle the numbers that can be divided by 5 with no remainder.

5   8   10   15   19   20   25   30   32   33   35   40   42

Flying Carpet

Name _____ Date _____

Solve the problems. ◆ If the answer is between 100 and 250, color the shape red. ◆ If the answer is between 251 and 900, color the shape blue. ◆ Finish the design by coloring the other shapes with the colors of your choice.

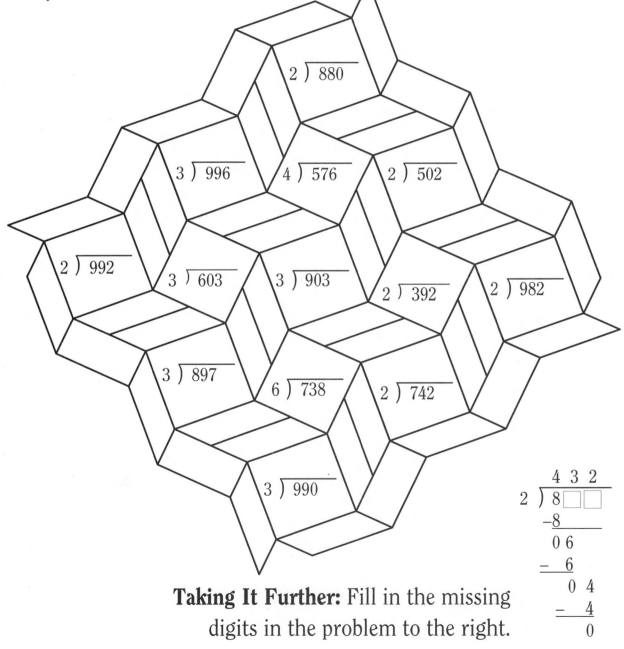

Taking It Further: Fill in the missing digits in the problem to the right.

$$
\begin{array}{r}
4\ 3\ 2 \\
2\,\overline{)\,8\ \square\ \square} \\
-8 \\
\hline
0\ 6 \\
-\ 6 \\
\hline
0\ 4 \\
-\ 4 \\
\hline
0
\end{array}
$$

Mathemagician

Name _____ Date _____

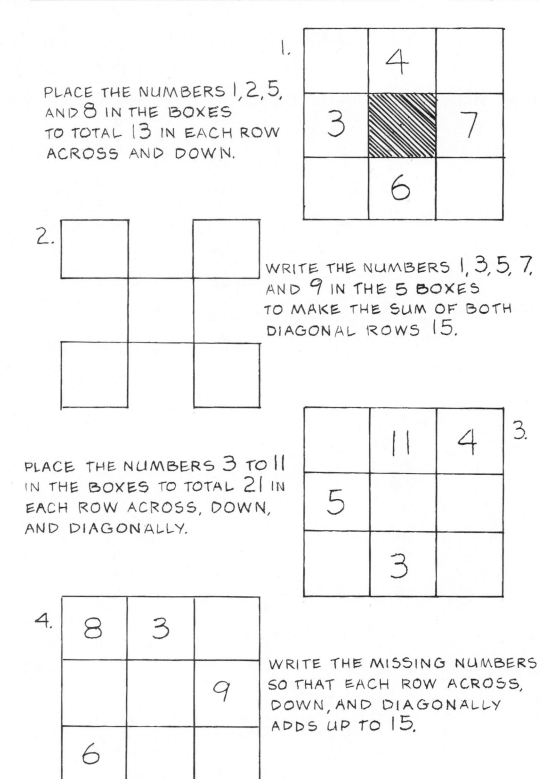

1.

PLACE THE NUMBERS 1, 2, 5, AND 8 IN THE BOXES TO TOTAL 13 IN EACH ROW ACROSS AND DOWN.

2.

WRITE THE NUMBERS 1, 3, 5, 7, AND 9 IN THE 5 BOXES TO MAKE THE SUM OF BOTH DIAGONAL ROWS 15.

PLACE THE NUMBERS 3 TO 11 IN THE BOXES TO TOTAL 21 IN EACH ROW ACROSS, DOWN, AND DIAGONALLY.

3.

4.

WRITE THE MISSING NUMBERS SO THAT EACH ROW ACROSS, DOWN, AND DIAGONALLY ADDS UP TO 15.

The Tree

Name _____ Date _____

Figure it out!

1. The apple that hit Rowena Pig fell from a branch that is 30 feet above the ground. How far is the branch from the top of the 100-foot tree?

_____

2. Rowena's ladder reaches up to 50 feet. How many feet shorter is the ladder than the 100-foot tree? _____

3. Starting on the ground, Itchy Squirrel climbs 20 feet up the tree. Then she stops to rest. She climbs 37 feet more and stops to rest again. How many feet did Itchy climb up the tree? _____

4. Rowena climbs 47 feet up the tree. Then an apple falls on her. The apple fell from a branch that is 92 feet up the tree. How many feet did the apple drop before hitting Rowena? _____

5. Itchy climbs 57 feet up the 100-foot tree. Then she climbs down 28 feet. How many feet is she from the top of the tree? _____

SUPER CHALLENGE: Itchy is 20 feet from the top of the 100-foot tree. She jumps straight across to a second tree. Now she's 30 feet from the top of the second tree. How tall is the second tree? _____

Who's Got the Button?

Name _____ Date _____

Figure it out!

1. If a button is lost every 3 seconds, how many buttons are lost in 60 seconds?

_____

2. Ant Betty finds some buttons. She gives 7 buttons to each of her 8 nieces. How many buttons did she find? _____

3. Molly Mouse organizes 6 groups of mice to look for lost buttons. Each group has 5 mice. How many mice are there in all? _____

4. One group of mice finds many buttons and they put them into 9 bags. Each bag contains 14 buttons. How many buttons did the mice find? _____

5. A second group of mice collects 20 bags containing a total of 160 buttons. Each bag contains the same number of buttons. How many buttons are in each bag? _____

SUPER CHALLENGE: Suppose 20 mice want to form teams with an equal number of mice on each team. How many different-size teams can they form?

Problems and More

Name _____ Date _____

Put on your thinking cap to solve these problems.

1. Magic Square

Using the numbers 1 to 9, fill in the squares so the rows across, down, and diagonally all add up to 15.

2. Pocket Change

I have 19 coins in my pocket. I have twice as many dimes as nickels, three more pennies than nickels, and one more dime than the number of pennies. My coins add up to $1.07. How many of each coin do I have?

_____ dimes

_____ nickels

_____ pennies

3. Connect the Dots

Can you connect all of the dots with four straight lines? Here's the catch: You can't lift your pencil or retrace a segment!

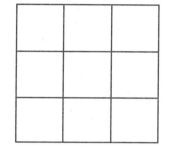

4. A Sneaky Puzzle

Something is hiding under your bed! To find out what it is, do this problem on a calculator:

5,000 + 45,842 + 2,203.

Turn the calculator upside down to reveal the answer.

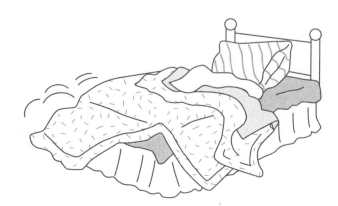

Problems and More

Name _____ Date _____

1. Tricky Triangles

How many triangles can you find
in this shape? Share ideas with
your classmates or family members.
Who found the most triangles?

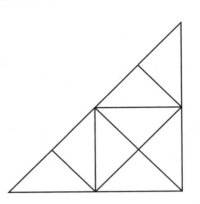

2. Time After Time

How are the clocks the same?
How are they different?

3. Half Again

Draw the missing half
of each shape.

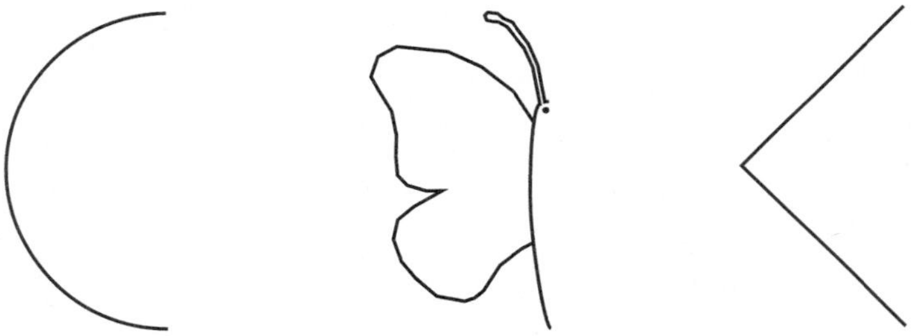

4. A Code for You!

ABC	DEF	GHI	JKL	MNO	PQR	STU	VWX	YZ
1	2	3	4	5	6	7	8	9

Use the code. Write your name. Then add to find the value of all the
letters in your name.

Name _____ Value _____

Find the value of some other words you know.

Brain Power!

Name _____ Date _____

Put on your thinking cap to solve these problems!

1. HOW MANY STUDENTS?

Estimate the number of students in your school. How did you do it?

_____

_____

_____

2. UPSIDE DOWN

What two-digit number reads the same upside down as it does right side up?

_____

3. CATS IN LINE

One cat walked in front of two cats. One cat walked behind two cats. One cat walked between two cats. How many cats were there? (Hint: Draw a picture!)

_____

4. NUMBER PATTERN

Here are the first five figures in a pattern. Draw the next figure.

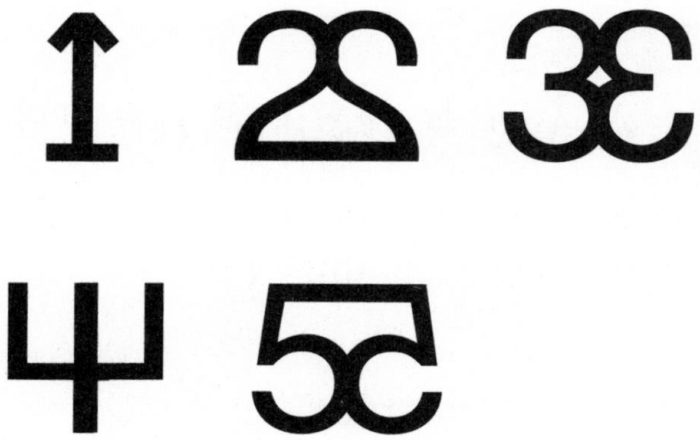

5. CUTTING THE CAKE!

What is the fewest number of cuts you could make in order to cut a cake into six slices? (Hint: Draw a picture!)

_____

Flag Wagger

Name _____   Date _____

Write a fraction for the section of the flag next to the arrow.

1. PANAMA

_____

2. NIGERIA

_____

3. MADAGASCAR

_____

4. MALTA

_____

5. POLAND

_____

6. MAURITIUS

_____

7. RUSSIA

_____

8. CHILE

_____

9. CZECH REPUBLIC

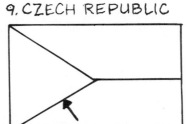

_____

10. TAIWAN

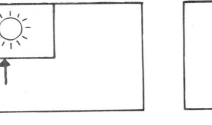

_____

11. UNITED ARAB EMIRATES

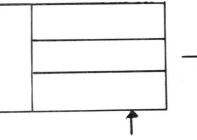

_____

12. MALAWI

Goody for Fractions!

Name _____ Date _____

Wash your hands, then gather the recipe ingredients and equipment listed below. To prepare the peanut butter–oatmeal drops, simply mix the ingredients together, roll the dough into balls, and place the balls on the wax paper. Chill the finished drops for about an hour, then enjoy your tasty "fractions" with family or friends!

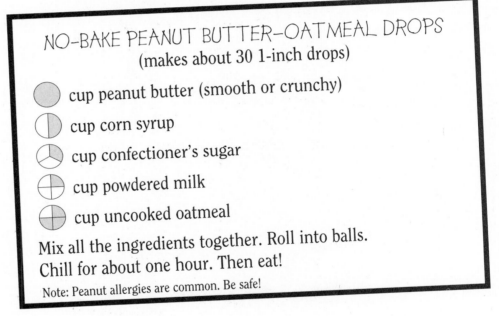

NO-BAKE PEANUT BUTTER–OATMEAL DROPS
(makes about 30 1-inch drops)

cup peanut butter (smooth or crunchy)

cup corn syrup

cup confectioner's sugar

cup powdered milk

cup uncooked oatmeal

Mix all the ingredients together. Roll into balls.
Chill for about one hour. Then eat!
Note: Peanut allergies are common. Be safe!

Now try these fraction pictures. Can you write the fraction each picture shows?

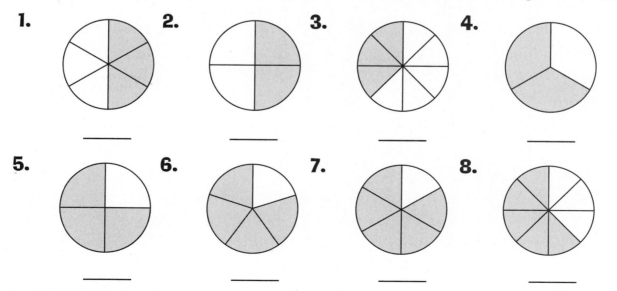

1. _____ 2. _____ 3. _____ 4. _____

5. _____ 6. _____ 7. _____ 8. _____

Flower Shop Fractions

Name _____   Date _____

Choose 2 colors for each bunch of flowers. Color some of the flowers one color. Color the rest of the flowers the other color. Write a fraction to tell how many flowers there are of each color.

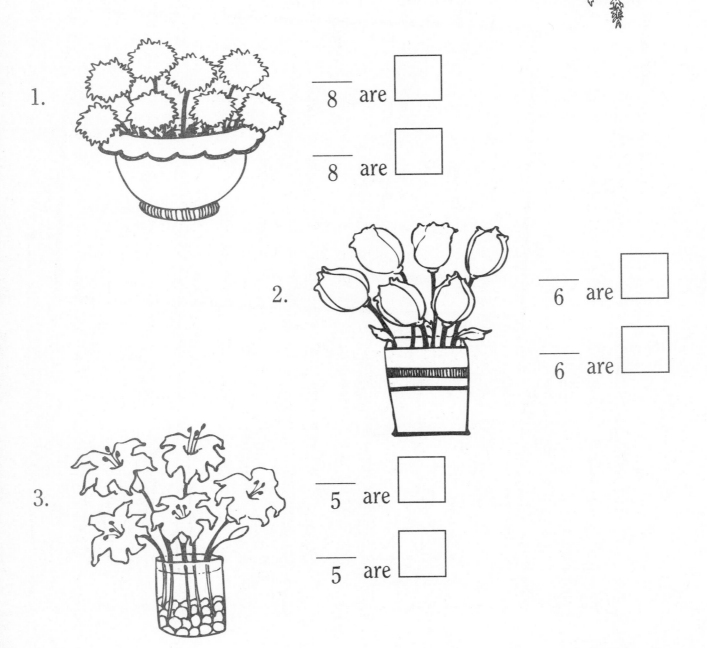

1.

$\dfrac{}{8}$ are ☐

$\dfrac{}{8}$ are ☐

2.

$\dfrac{}{6}$ are ☐

$\dfrac{}{6}$ are ☐

3.

$\dfrac{}{5}$ are ☐

$\dfrac{}{5}$ are ☐

Handy Dandy Fraction Candy

Name _____ Date _____

Use these candy bars to see just how sweet fractions can be!

You Need:
scissors

What to Do:

- Cut out the candy bars along the dashed lines.
- Work with a partner. Use both candy bars to do the activity.

1. Arrange some of the pieces this way to make a whole bar:

   Here's how you can show that combination of fractions in an equation:

   $\frac{1}{2} + \frac{1}{4} + \frac{1}{6} + \frac{1}{12} = 1$ whole candy bar

2. Can you find another way to make one whole candy bar without using the $\frac{1}{2}$ piece? What would it look like? How would you write it in a fraction equation?

3. How many ways can you use the pieces to make whole candy bars? (Each whole bar will have 12 pieces.) Draw a picture of each solution on a separate sheet of paper.

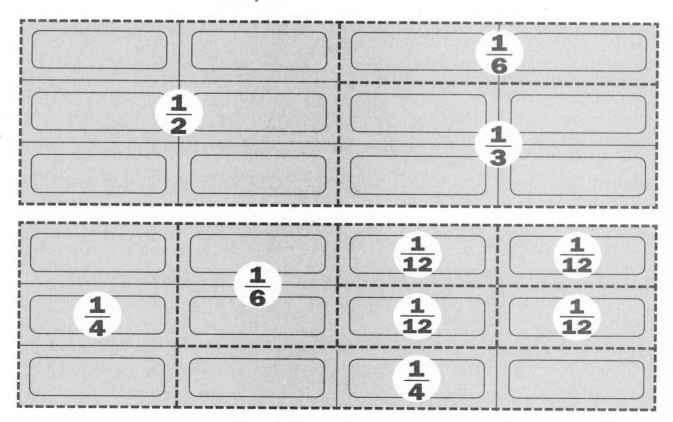

41

Cooking With Fractions

Name _____ Date _____

The recipe below explains how to make peanut-butter balls.
Read the recipe. Then answer the questions.

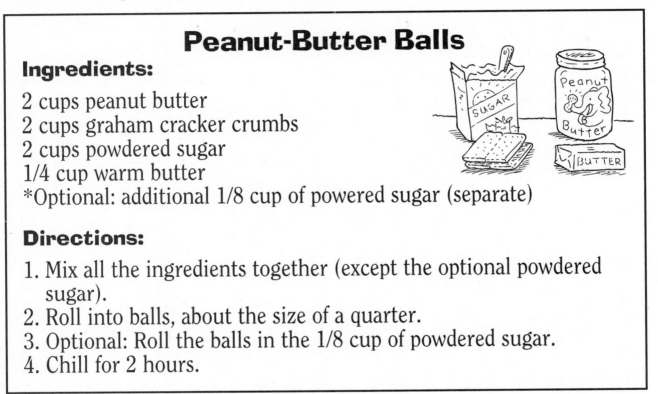

Peanut-Butter Balls

Ingredients:

2 cups peanut butter
2 cups graham cracker crumbs
2 cups powdered sugar
1/4 cup warm butter
*Optional: additional 1/8 cup of powered sugar (separate)

Directions:

1. Mix all the ingredients together (except the optional powdered sugar).
2. Roll into balls, about the size of a quarter.
3. Optional: Roll the balls in the 1/8 cup of powdered sugar.
4. Chill for 2 hours.

Several classmates want to help make the peanut-butter balls.

1. How many students would be needed if each measured 1/2 cup of the peanut butter?

   _____

2. How many students would be needed if each measured 1/4 cup of the graham cracker crumbs?

   _____

3. How many students would be needed if each measured 1/3 cup of the powdered sugar?

   _____

Into Infinity

Name _____ Date _____

Solve the problems. Then rename the answers in lowest terms.

If the answer is $\frac{1}{4}$, $\frac{1}{8}$, or $\frac{1}{16}$, color the shape purple.

If the answer is $\frac{1}{2}$, $\frac{1}{3}$, or $\frac{1}{7}$, color the shape blue.

If the answer is $\frac{2}{3}$, $\frac{3}{4}$, or $\frac{7}{8}$, color the shape green.

If the answer is $\frac{3}{5}$, $\frac{4}{5}$, or $\frac{5}{7}$, color the shape yellow.

If the answer is $\frac{9}{10}$ or $\frac{11}{12}$, color the shape red.

Finish the design by coloring the other shapes with colors of your choice.

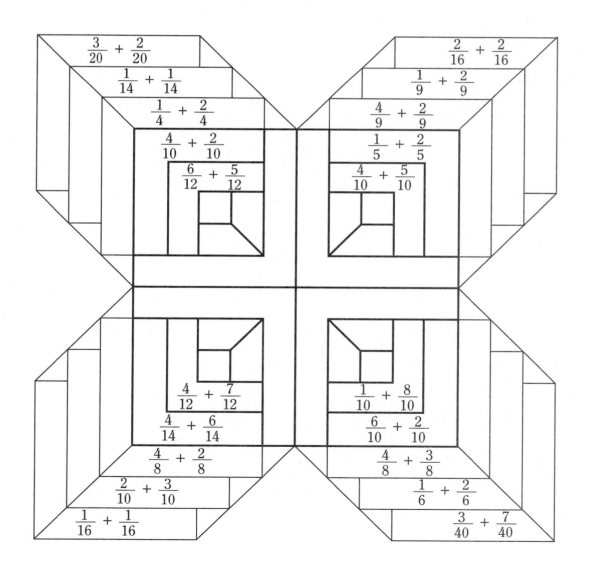

Kaleidoscope of Flowers

Name _____ Date _____

If the number has a 5 in the ones place, color the shape green.
If the number has a 5 in the tenths place, color the shape pink.
If the number has a 5 in the hundredths place, color the shape yellow.
Finish the design by coloring the other shapes with colors of your choice.

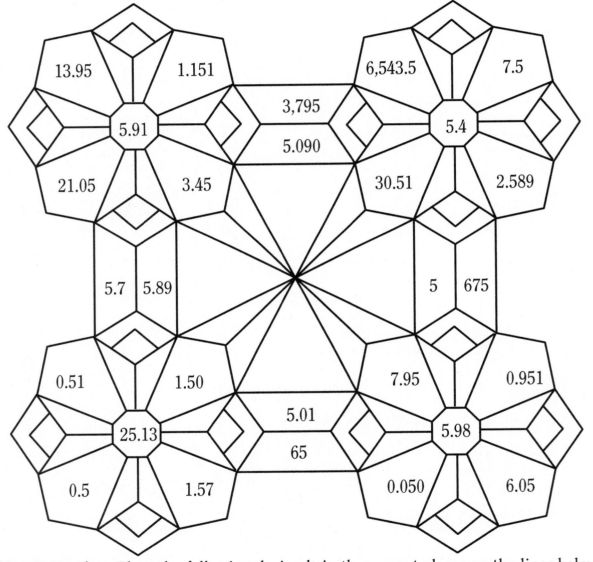

Taking It Further: Place the following decimals in the correct places on the lines below the dots: 4.9, 1.7, 2.5, and 0.2.

Put the Brakes on Math Mistakes!

Name _____ Date _____

Take a look at the signs on Bob's store. Circle any mistakes you see.
Then fix the mistakes so that the signs are correct.

BOB'S BIKE BARN

Bike Helmets
$14.999

OPEN
9:30 AM - 8:75 PM

OPEN
8 DAYS
A WEEK

* SALE *
$10 off selected
Mountain Bikes
Were $139.99
Now $129.00

Handlebar Tape
$3.99 a roll,
Buy two for $7.97
SAVE $1.00

Bicycle Baskets
$12.99 each
Two for $25.00
SAVE $.98

* FREE *
Bicycle
Stickers
$.10 each

Bicycle Chain
$.50 an inch
That's only $5.00 a foot

½ off all
Bicycle seats
Were $17.00
Now $9.50

45

Autumn Harvest

Name _____ Date _____

Circle the coins that you need to pay for each thing in the picture on page 47.

Dollar Scholar

Name _____ Date _____

How many ways can you make a dollar? Write the number of coins you will need.

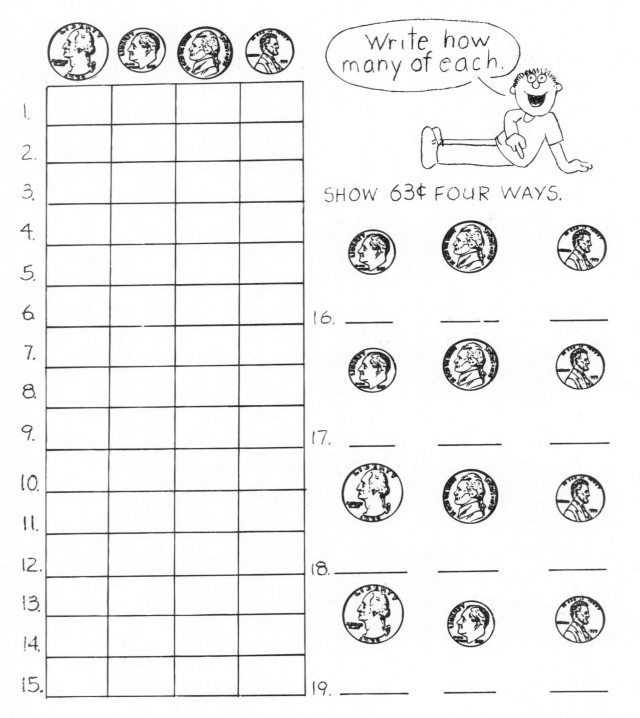

Write how many of each.

SHOW 63¢ FOUR WAYS.

1.
2.
3.
4.
5.
6.
7.
8.
9.
10.
11.
12.
13.
14.
15.

16. ____ ____ ____

17. ____ ____ ____

18. ____ ____ ____

19. ____ ____ ____

Time for a Riddle!

Name _____   Date _____

Read the riddle. To find the answer, find the clockface that matches the time written under each blank line. Then write the letter under that clockface on the blank line.

Riddle: What did the little hand on the clock say to the big hand?

Answer: " ____   ____   ____   ____   ____   ____   ____
           10:00   3:30   3:30   6:05   2:25   3:45   6:15

           ____   ____   ____   ____   ____   ____ !"
           4:45   6:05   2:55   3:45   3:45   2:55

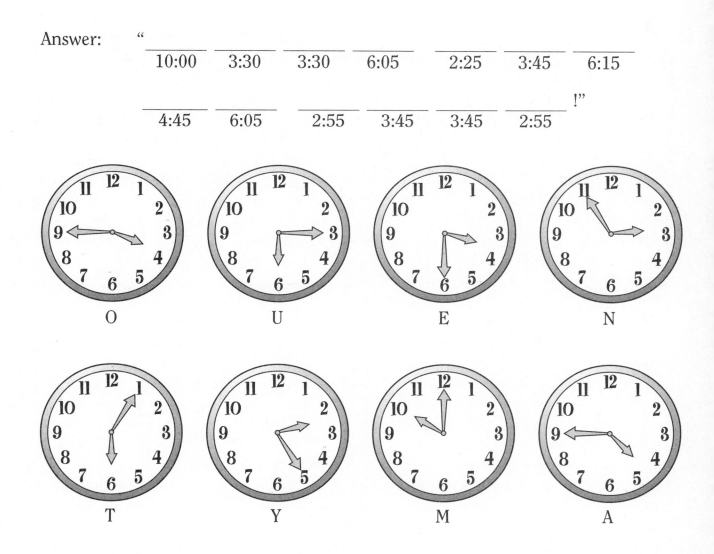

Curves Ahead!

Name _____ Date _____

How long is each curved line? Guess. Then check by measuring.

1. My guess _____

Actual length _____

2. My guess _____

Actual length _____

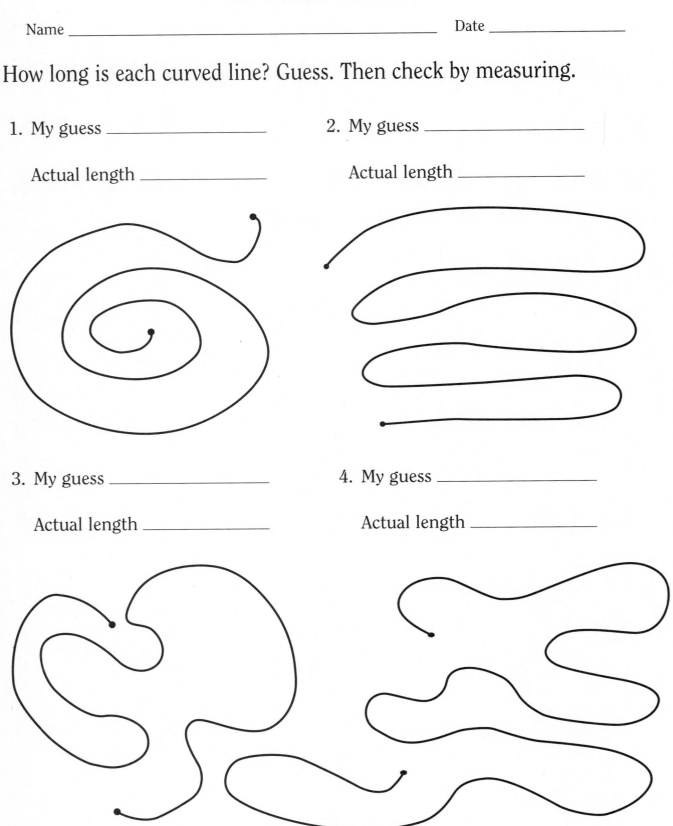

3. My guess _____

Actual length _____

4. My guess _____

Actual length _____

50

Measure With Me

Name _____ Date _____

Cut a piece of string or yarn that is equal to your height. Measure each object below and check the correct box.

Object	Longer than my string	Shorter than my string	The same as my string

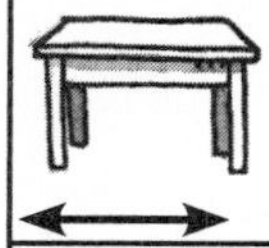			

◎ Measure something else. Draw a picture of it on another piece of paper. Write a sentence to show what you found out.

_____

_____

◎ Have someone measure you. Who measured you? _____
How tall are you? _____

Weight Watcher

Name _____   Date _____

Weight can be measured in ounces (oz.) and pounds (lb.). 16 oz. = 1 lb.
Which unit of measure would you use to weigh the items below?
Underline the more sensible measure.

1. An apple

     ounces   pounds

2. A pair of boots

     ounces   pounds

3. A bar of soap

     ounces   pounds

4. A bicycle

     ounces   pounds

5. A watermelon

     ounces   pounds

6. A baseball player

     ounces   pounds

7. A balloon

     ounces   pounds

8. A jam sandwich

     ounces   pounds

9. A baseball bat

     ounces   pounds

10. A pair of socks

     ounces   pounds

11. A slice of pizza

     ounces   pounds

12. A full backpack

     ounces   pounds

13. A large dog

     ounces   pounds

14. A loaf of bread

     ounces   pounds

15. A paintbrush

     ounces   pounds

Degree Overseer

Name _____ Date _____

Temperature is measured in degrees. Fahrenheit (°F) is a common measure in the U.S. Celsius (°C) is a metric measure. Circle the more sensible temperature in which to do the activities below.

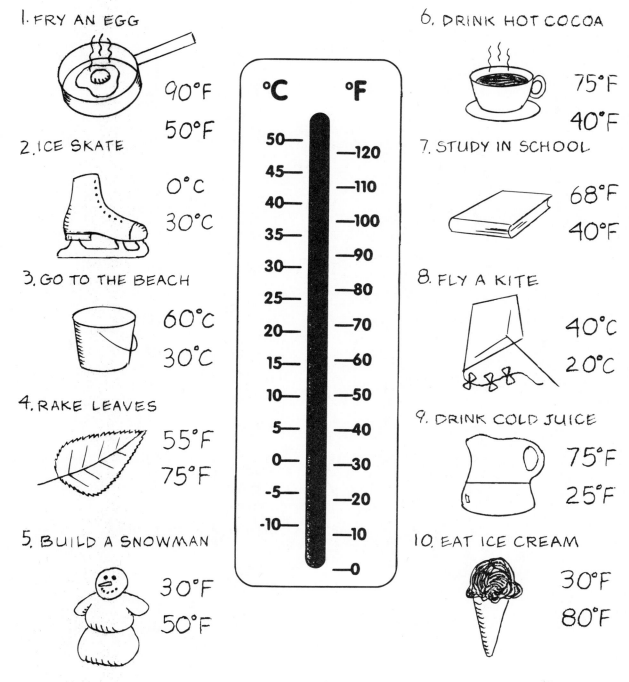

1. FRY AN EGG

90°F
50°F

2. ICE SKATE

0°C
30°C

3. GO TO THE BEACH

60°C
30°C

4. RAKE LEAVES

55°F
75°F

5. BUILD A SNOWMAN

30°F
50°F

6. DRINK HOT COCOA

75°F
40°F

7. STUDY IN SCHOOL

68°F
40°F

8. FLY A KITE

40°C
20°C

9. DRINK COLD JUICE

75°F
25°F

10. EAT ICE CREAM

30°F
80°F

°C   °F

50—   —120
45—   —110
40—   —100
35—   —90
30—   —80
25—
20—   —70
15—   —60
10—   —50
5—   —40
0—   —30
-5—   —20
-10—   —10
           —0

Fact Finder

Name _____ Date _____

Numbers can be used to count and to measure. Complete the measures below by writing how many are in each.

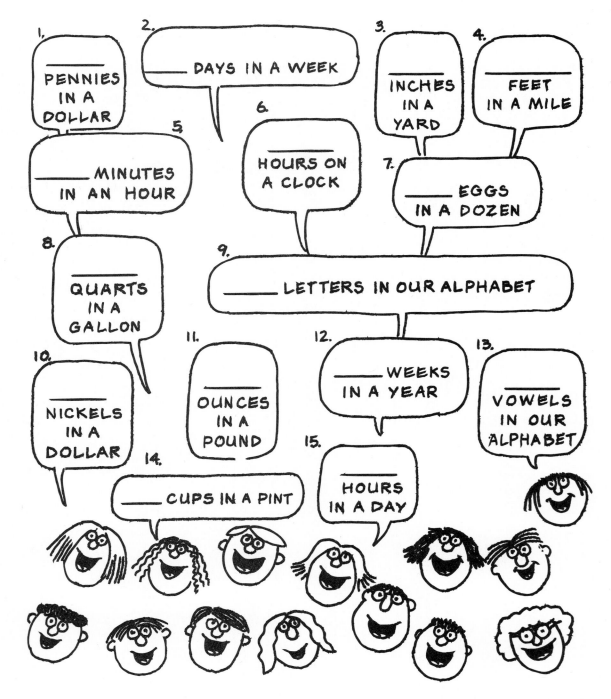

1. _____ PENNIES IN A DOLLAR

2. _____ DAYS IN A WEEK

3. _____ INCHES IN A YARD

4. _____ FEET IN A MILE

5. _____ MINUTES IN AN HOUR

6. _____ HOURS ON A CLOCK

7. _____ EGGS IN A DOZEN

8. _____ QUARTS IN A GALLON

9. _____ LETTERS IN OUR ALPHABET

10. _____ NICKELS IN A DOLLAR

11. _____ OUNCES IN A POUND

12. _____ WEEKS IN A YEAR

13. _____ VOWELS IN OUR ALPHABET

14. _____ CUPS IN A PINT

15. _____ HOURS IN A DAY

Amount Counter

Name _____ Date _____

How many triangles and squares can you count in these geometric figures?

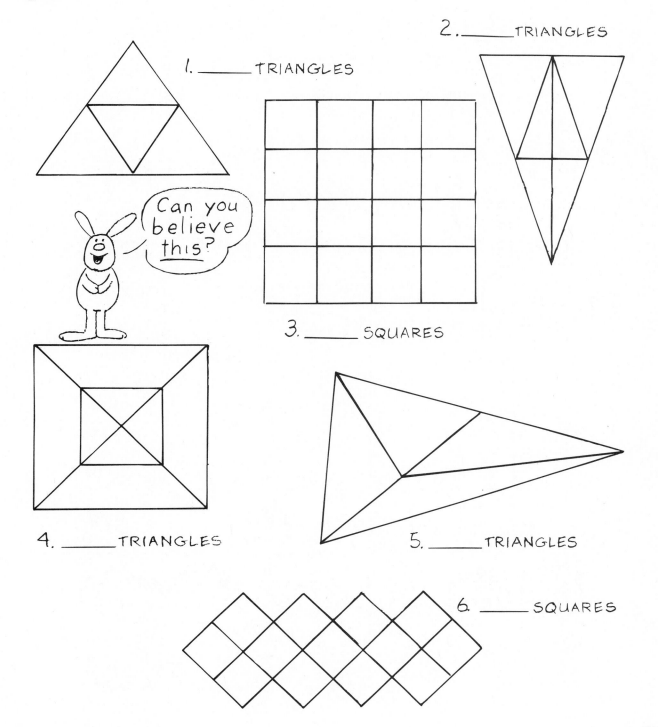

1. _____ TRIANGLES

2. _____ TRIANGLES

3. _____ SQUARES

4. _____ TRIANGLES

5. _____ TRIANGLES

6. _____ SQUARES

Can you believe this?

55

Shape Gaper

Name _____ Date _____

FLAT SHAPES HAVE LENGTH AND WIDTH.

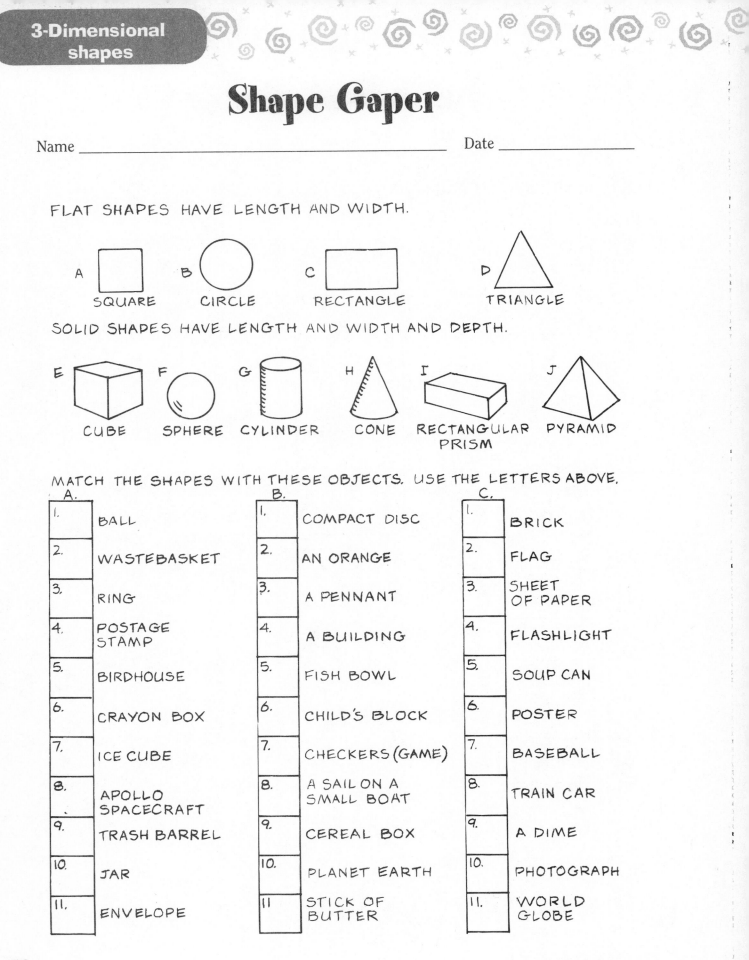

A □ SQUARE   B ○ CIRCLE   C ▭ RECTANGLE   D △ TRIANGLE

SOLID SHAPES HAVE LENGTH AND WIDTH AND DEPTH.

E CUBE   F SPHERE   G CYLINDER   H CONE   I RECTANGULAR PRISM   J PYRAMID

MATCH THE SHAPES WITH THESE OBJECTS. USE THE LETTERS ABOVE.

A.
1. BALL
2. WASTEBASKET
3. RING
4. POSTAGE STAMP
5. BIRDHOUSE
6. CRAYON BOX
7. ICE CUBE
8. APOLLO SPACECRAFT
9. TRASH BARREL
10. JAR
11. ENVELOPE

B.
1. COMPACT DISC
2. AN ORANGE
3. A PENNANT
4. A BUILDING
5. FISH BOWL
6. CHILD'S BLOCK
7. CHECKERS (GAME)
8. A SAIL ON A SMALL BOAT
9. CEREAL BOX
10. PLANET EARTH
11. STICK OF BUTTER

C.
1. BRICK
2. FLAG
3. SHEET OF PAPER
4. FLASHLIGHT
5. SOUP CAN
6. POSTER
7. BASEBALL
8. TRAIN CAR
9. A DIME
10. PHOTOGRAPH
11. WORLD GLOBE

Riddle Teller

Name _____ Date _____

Read the riddle. Then draw the shape it describes.

I have 3 sides and 3 corners. One of my corners is at the top.

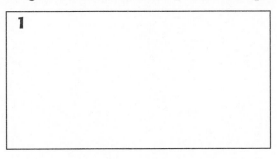

1

I have no corners. One half of me is like the other half.

2

I have 4 corners and 4 sides. You can draw me by joining 2 triangles.

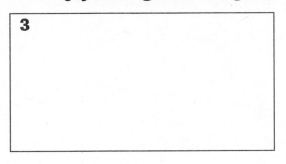

3

I have 5 sides and 5 corners. Draw a square and a triangle together.

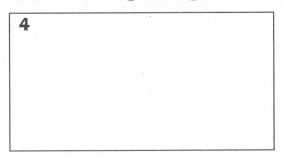

4

I am not a square, but I have 4 sides and 4 corners.

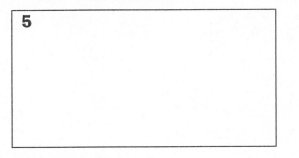

5

I have 4 sides and 4 corners. My 2 opposite sides are slanted.

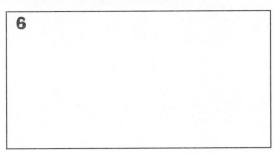

6

Pattern Block Design

Name _____ Date _____

How many total pieces are in this pattern block design?

2 + 2 + 2 + 4 = _____

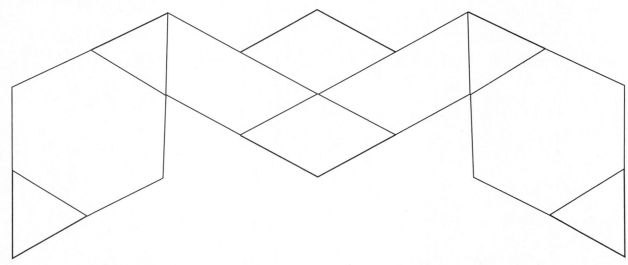

Now make your own design. Use 10 pattern blocks different from those used above. Cut out the shapes and trace or glue them in the space below. You may need to use a shape more than once.

Write an equation to show how many of each shape you used.

Equation: _____

Don't Wait—Tessellate!

Find how easy it is to make beautiful tiled patterns.

Preparation

Mark and cut the cardboard into 3-inch by 3-inch squares.

Directions

Here are the steps in creating a tessellation.

1. Draw a simple shape on one side of the square. Some ideas:

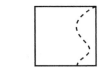

2. Cut out the shape, slide it directly to the opposite side of the square (don't turn it or flip it), and tape the straight sides together.

3. Repeat the process on one of the remaining sides. The tessellation template is complete.

4. Trace the template in any spot on the construction paper. Slide the template in any direction (don't turn it or flip it), match the template with the first tracing, and trace it again. Repeat the process until the page is covered.

5. Color the tessellation in any way. Decorate the shapes to bring out patterns of animals, people, flowers, or designs.

You'll Need

◆ Lightweight cardboard or oak tag
◆ Scissors and tape
◆ Crayons and construction paper (in a light shade)
◆ Pencils

Answer Key

Page 5

1. 9; **2.** 22; **3.** 17; **4.** 45; **5.** 67
6. 108; **7.** 86; **8.** 153; **9.** 370; **10.** 534

Where do cows go for entertainment?

To the "moo"vies

Page 6-7

Scores will vary.

Page 8

Answers will vary.

Page 9

A. thousands; **B.** tens; **C.** hundreds; **D.** tens
E. hundreds; **F.** ones; **G.** tens
The answer to the riddle is "a secret."

Page 10

1. 10; **2.** 20; **3.** 50; **4.** 90; **5.** 200
6. 400; **7.** 600; **8.** 300; **9.** 500; **10.** 700

What did the farmer get when he tried to reach the beehive?

A "buzzy" signal

Page 11

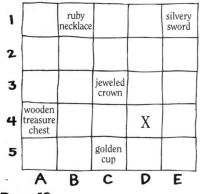

Page 12

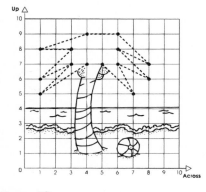

Page 13

1. cheetah; **2.** black mamba snake; **3.** zebra
4. lion; **5.** 7; **6.** yes; **7.** speed; **8.** no

Page 14

Check graphs for each.

5 pennies equal 5 cents, one nickel equals 5 cents

10 pennies equal 10 cents, 2 nickels equal 10 cents,
 one dime equals 10 cents

25 pennies equal 25 cents, 5 nickels equal 25 cents,
 one quarter equals 25 cents

Page 15

1. Jan and Dec; **2.** 80° **3.** June, July, and Sept; **4.** Yes; 10° **5.** No
6. Warmer **7.** Fall **8.** May **9.** 40 degrees

Pages 16–17

1. Tortillas and Eggs; Chinese Breakfast Rice **2.** $5.50 **3.** $6.00
4. Jack; 50¢ more **5.** Tortillas and Eggs **6.** Answers will vary.

Page 18

Page 19

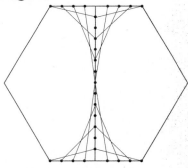

Taking It Further: 7 flowers

Page 20

A CLOCK
$60 - 34 = 26$; $52 - 38 = 14$; $64 - 29 = 35$
ON DECK
$44 - 28 = 16$; $51 - 26 = 25$; $70 - 36 = 34$
A CRANE
$41 - 29 = 12$; $64 - 28 = 36$; $81 - 36 = 45$
SILENCE
$80 - 49 = 31$; $91 - 49 = 42$; $92 - 36 = 56$

Page 21

779 – 197 = 582; 822 – 187 = 635; 242 – 133 = 109
704 – 315 = 389; 745 – 219 = 526; 912 – 119 = 793
643 – 250 = 393; 727 – 533 = 194; 743 – 146 = 597
829 – 147 = 682; 725 – 137 = 588; 698 – 119 = 579
935 – 149 = 786; 904 – 183 = 721; 862 – 170 = 692
795 – 106 = 689; 401 – 298 = 103; 874 – 486 = 388
684 – 136 = 548; 721 – 155 = 566; 724 – 473 = 251
542 – 368 = 174; 884 – 275 = 609; 987 – 396 = 591
Taking It Further: 973 – 379 = 594

Page 22

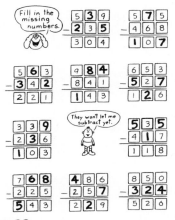

Page 23

345 – 186 = 159; 879 – 580 = 299; 635 – 241 = 394;
977 – 418 = 559; 648 – 109 = 539; 492 – 127 = 365;
628 – 329 = 299; 863 – 148 = 715; 544 – 261 = 283;
860 – 732 = 128; 900 – 119 = 781; 969 – 380 = 589

Page 24

1. 12; **2.** 24; **3.** 8; **4.** 36; **5.** 28
6. 40; **7.** 32; **8.** 52; **9.** 4; **10.** 48
What does a basketball player never have to pay for?
A "free" throw

Page 25

Page 26

YOUR SMILE
6 x 1 = 6; 6 x 4 = 24; 7 x 7 = 49; 6 x 2 = 12
7 x 9 = 63; 6 x 3 = 18; 7 x 3 = 21; 7 x 6 = 42
7 x 4 = 28; 6 x 5 = 30; 6 x 6 = 36; 6 x 9 = 54
7 x 8 = 56; 7 x 0 = 0; 6 x 7 = 42; 6 x 0 = 0
7 x 5 = 35; 6 x 8 = 48; 7 x 2 = 14; 7 x 1 = 7

Page 27

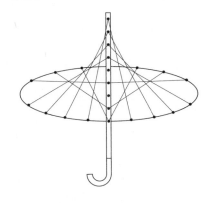

Taking It Further: a. 11 **b.** 10 **c.** 0 **d.** 3 **e.** 4 **f.** 12

Page 28

6 x 1 = 6; 6 x 4 = 24; 7 x 6 = 42; 11 x 7 = 77
7 x 8 = 56; 10 x 6 = 60; 8 x 6 = 48; 7 x 7 = 49
12 x 7 = 84; 6 x 3 = 18; 7 x 5 = 35; 5 x 6 = 30
6 x 7 = 42; 7 x 1 = 7; 7 x 3 = 21; 10 x 7 = 70
11 x 6 = 66; 7 x 9 = 63; 6 x 9 = 54; 12 x 6 = 72
7 x 9 = 63; 6 x 6 = 36; 2 x 7 = 14; 4 x 7 = 28
Taking It Further: 8 x 49 = 392

Page 29

1. 9R1; **2.** 3R3
3. 4R0; **4.** 5R0
5. 2R0; **6.** 6R1
7. 3R0; **8.** 9R2
9. 6R0; **10.** 4R3

Page 30

35 ÷ 5 = 7; 55 ÷ 5 = 11; 30 ÷ 5 = 6
15 ÷ 5 = 3; 10 ÷ 5 = 2; 45 ÷ 5 = 9
15 ÷ 5 = 3; 5 ÷ 5 = 1; 25 ÷ 5 = 5
20 ÷ 5 = 4; 25 ÷ 5 = 5; 40 ÷ 5 = 8
45 ÷ 5 = 9; 5 ÷ 5 = 1
Taking It Further: 5, 10, 15, 20, 25, 30, 35, 40

Page 31

880 ÷ 2 = 440; 996 ÷ 3 = 332; 576 ÷ 4 = 144
502 ÷ 2 = 251; 992 ÷ 2 = 496; 603 ÷ 3 = 201
903 ÷ 3 = 301; 392 ÷ 2 = 196; 982 ÷ 2 = 491
897 ÷ 3 = 299; 738 ÷ 6 = 123; 742 ÷ 2 = 371
990 ÷ 3 = 330
Taking It Further:

```
        4 3 2
    2 ) 8 6 4
      -  8
         0 6
       -   6
           0 4
         -   4
             0
```

Page 32

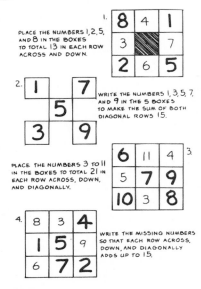

PLACE THE NUMBERS 1, 2, 5, AND 8 IN THE BOXES TO TOTAL 13 IN EACH ROW ACROSS AND DOWN.

WRITE THE NUMBERS 1, 3, 5, 7, AND 9 IN THE 5 BOXES TO MAKE THE SUM OF BOTH DIAGONAL ROWS 15.

PLACE THE NUMBERS 3 TO 11 IN THE BOXES TO TOTAL 21 IN EACH ROW ACROSS, DOWN, AND DIAGONALLY.

WRITE THE MISSING NUMBERS SO THAT EACH ROW ACROSS, DOWN, AND DIAGONALLY ADDS UP TO 15.

Page 33
1. 70 feet
2. 50 feet
3. 57 feet
4. 45 feet
5. 71 feet
Super Challenge: 110 feet

Page 34
1. 20 buttons; **2.** 56 buttons; **3.** 30 mice
4. 126 buttons; **5.** 8 buttons
Super Challenge: 6 teams

Page 35
1. Here is one way to complete the square. (Students may invert the rows and columns.)

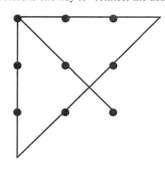

2. 8 dimes, 4 nickels, and 7 pennies
3. Here is one way to "connect the dots":

4. ShOES (53045)

Page 36
1. 17 triangles
2. They show the same time in different ways.
3. Children should complete the shapes.
4. Answers will vary.

Page 37
1. Answers will vary. Sample answers: Students may take an average class size of 30 students and multiply 30 by the number of classes in the school.
2. Answers include 11, 88, 69, and 96.
3. 3 cats
4.

5. three cuts

Page 38
1. 1/4; **2.** 1/3; **3.** 1/3; **4.** 1/2; **5.** 1/2
6. 1/4; **7.** 1/3; **8.** 1/2; **9.** 1/4; **10.** 1/4
11. 1/4; **12.** 1/3

Page 39
1. 3/6; **2.** 2/4; **3.** 3/8; **4.** 2/3
5. 3/4; **6.** 4/5; **7.** 5/6; **8.** 5/8

Page 40
Answers will vary.

Page 41
Here are six ways to make whole candy bars out of the fraction pieces. Your students may find more.

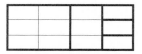

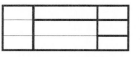

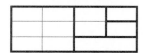

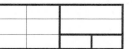

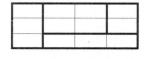

Page 42
1. 4 students; **2.** 8 students; **3.** 6 students

Page 43

3/20 + 2/20 = 1/4; 2/16 + 2/16 = 1/4; 1/14 + 1/14 = 1/7
1/9 + 2/9 = 1/3; 1/4 + 2/4 = 3/4; 4/ 9 + 2/9 = 2/3
4/10 + 2/10 = 3/5; 1/5 + 2/5 = 3/5; 6/12 + 5/12 = 11/12
4/10 + 5/10 = 9/10; 4/12 + 7/12 = 11/12; 1/10 + 8/10 = 9/10
4/14 + 6/14 = 5/7; 6/10 + 2/10 = 4/5; 4/8 + 2/8 = 3/4
4/8 + 3/8 = 7/8; 2/10 + 3/10 = 1/2; 1/6 + 2/6 = 1/2
1/16 + 1/16 = 1/8; 3/40 + 7/40 = 1/4

Page 44

Check students' work.
Taking It Further:

Page 45

Check that students have found all of the mistakes and that they have fixed the mistakes with reasonable corrections. **Mistakes:** 8 days a week should be 7; 8:75 pm is not possible; $10.99 off mountain bikes; bicycle chain is $6.00 a foot; bike helmets are $14.99; you save only $.01, not $1.00, on 2 rolls of tape; free stickers can't be 10 cents each; half-price bicycle seats should be $8.50.
The additional mistake—a clock with three hands.

Pages 46-47

apple: 5 pennies
jelly: 2 dimes **or** 1 dime + 2 nickels
cider: 1 quarter + 1 nickel
corn: 3 dimes + 1 nickel **or** 2 dimes + 3 nickels
pumpkin: 1 quarter + 2 dimes **or** 1 quarter + 1 dime + 2 nickels
squash: 1 quarter + 2 dimes + 1 nickel
pie: 1 quarter + 1 dime + 1 nickel
hay ride: 2 dimes + 1 nickel **or** 2 dimes + 5 pennies

Page 48

Page 49

Answer: "Meet you at noon!"

Page 50

The actual measurements will vary somewhat, but they should be close to the following:
1. 14 1/2 inches
2. 19 inches
3. 13 1/2 inches
4. 21 inches

Page 51

Answers will vary.

Page 52

1. ounces; **2.** pounds; **3.** ounces; **4.** pounds
5. pounds; **6.** pounds; **7.** ounces; **8.** ounces
9. pounds; **10.** ounces; **11.** ounces; **12.** pounds
13. pounds; **14.** ounces; **15.** ounces

Page 53

1. 90°F; **2.** 0°C; **3.** 30°C; **4.** 55°F; **5.** 30°F
6. 40°F; **7.** 68°F; **8.** 20°C; **9.** 75°F; **10.** 80°F

Page 54

1. 100; **2.** 7; **3.** 36; **4.** 5280; **5.** 60
6. 12; **7.** 12; **8.** 4; **9.** 26; **10.** 20
11. 16; **12.** 52; **13.** 5; **14.** 2; **15.** 24

Page 55

1. 5; **2.** 11; **3.** 30; **4.** 12; **5.** 8; **6.** 17

Page 56

A. 1. F, 2. G, 3. B, 4. C or A, 5. E, 6. I, 7. E, 8. H, 9. G, 10. G, 11. C
B. 1. B, 2. F, 3. D, 4. I, 5. F, 6. E, 7. A, 8. D, 9. I, 10. F, 11. I
C. 1. I, 2. C, 3. C, 4. G, 5. G, 6. C, 7. F, 8. I, 9. B, 10. C or A, 11. F

Page 57

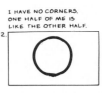

I HAVE 3 SIDES AND 3 CORNERS. ONE OF MY CORNERS IS AT THE TOP.

I HAVE NO CORNERS. ONE HALF OF ME IS LIKE THE OTHER HALF.

I HAVE 4 CORNERS AND 4 SIDES. YOU CAN DRAW ME BY JOINING 2 TRIANGLES.

I HAVE 5 SIDES AND 5 CORNERS. DRAW A SQUARE AND A TRIANGLE TOGETHER.

I AM NOT A SQUARE BUT I HAVE 4 SIDES AND 4 CORNERS.

I HAVE 4 SIDES AND 4 CORNERS. MY 2 OPPOSITE SIDES ARE SLANTED.

Page 58

10; answers will vary.

Page 59

Children's tessellate patterns will vary.

Instant Skills Index